PIANO DUETS

RODGERS AND HAMMERSTEIN™

Arranged for Piano Duet, One Piano Four Hands by DAVID CARR GLOVER

Foreword

These ten songs from THE SOUND OF MUSIC have been arranged for piano duet, one piano four hands. The original rhythms have not been altered and for the most part, the original chord structure is the same, though simplified.

Contents

WILLIAMSON MUSIC®

A RODGERS AND HAMMERSTEIN COMPANY

EXCLUSIVELY DISTRIBUTED BY

HAL•LEONARD® CORPORATION

7777 W. BLUEMOUND RD. P.O. BOX 13819 MILWAUKEE, WI 53213

Applications for performance of this work, whether legitimate, stock,
amateur, or foreign, should be addressed to:
THE RODGERS AND HAMMERSTEIN THEATRE LIBRARY
229 West 28th Street, 11th Floor; New York, NY 10001
Telephone: (212)564-4000; Facsimile: (212)268-1245

ISBN 0-7935-0758-8

Mary Martin with the Trapp children singing "Do-Re-Mi".

THE SOUND OF MUSIC ®

What, tragically, turned out to be the last musical play produced by the legendary Rodgers and Hammerstein team has become one of their most successful and well-loved, both here and abroad. The show opened in New York on November 16, 1959, and ran there for over three and a half years. The National Company toured with it for nearly three years more, and there have been numerous revivals. Oscar Hammerstein was never to learn how utterly his last lyrics had been taken to the hearts of his countrymen. He died at his home in Doylestown, Pennsylvania, on August 23, 1960, one of the most respected — as he was one of the most loved — figures in the history of the American theatre.

Hammerstein's essential sweetness of character was reflected in the subjects he chose to adapt for the musical stage. Shortly before he began his adaptation of Baroness Maria von Trapp's autobiographical *The Trapp Family Singers* as the basis for *The Sound Of Music*, he was offered a best-selling, highly romantic account of the life of the senior Alexandre Dumas. It was a story that seemed, superficially, to be specially tailored for the Rodgers and Hammerstein talents. But he turned it down, explaining, "Basically, the man isn't decent enough. Dick and I like to work with good people — ones we wouldn't mind having around the place for months." There had to be occasional villains, of course, but even the most obviously malodorous villain, Jud in *Oklahoma!*, is somehow malodorous in an endearing way. The villain in *The Sound Of Music* is the Nazi party and the evil of *Anschluss,* which causes the Trapp family to exile themselves from their beloved Austria in the end. It is significant that the one important member of the cast who turns out to have been a Nazi all along — Rolf Gruber, the young suitor of the Trapps' eldest daughter — finally deceives his superiors and makes possible his beloved's escape with her family. In a Rodgers and Hammerstein play, even the representative of pure evil is likely to perform redeeming acts.

In the play, as in life, the Baron Georg von Trapp had been a Captain in the Imperial Austrian Navy and had had a distinguished record.

Many thousands of Americans will recall how this middle-aged gentleman with the military bearing used to appear on stage at the end of his family's concerts of vocal and instrumental music.

It was a highly gifted and well-disciplined group, and among the most welcome and constructive refugees from Hitler ever to come to these shores. But the central figure in the play is not the Baron, but Maria Rainer — played by Mary Martin in the original Broadway production and by Julie Andrews in the motion picture — a postulant at Nonnberg Abbey when we meet her. A quicksilvery character, she is loved by all the sisters, but they find her all but uncontrollable ("How do you hold a moonbeam in your hands?" they ask). And indeed, when we first see the music-loving outdoor girl, she is off by herself in the lovely Austrian countryside singing, "The hills are alive with the sound of music," so entranced with her surroundings that inevitably she is late again in returning to the Abbey. Obviously such an indomitable free spirit is not yet ready to enter the novitiate as so many of her fellow postulant nuns are about to do. In an interview with the compassionate Mother Abbess, Maria ingenuously explains how she keeps up her spirits by thinking of her favorite things:

Cream-colored ponies and crisp apple strudels,
Doorbells and sleigh bells and schnitzel with noodles...

It is a song the Mother Abbess herself has known since childhood, and she joins the young postulant in singing it.

The retired naval captain turns out to be a man embittered by the death of his wife, who spends much of his time away from his beautiful estate, returning only when the current governess leaves and he must engage a new one. This seems to be a frequent occurrence, for the Captain runs his home and his family of five girls and two boys with whistles, as if it were his ship and they its crew. Every morning the children — ranging in age from a toddler to an adolescent girl almost Maria's age — must have their lessons, and every after-

Mary Martin, Theodore Bikel and the Trapp children on stage in the Broadway production of "The Sound Of Music".

THE SOUND OF MUSIC ®

noon they must march. No singing. But Maria will have none of this. She throws away the whistle supplied by the Captain and, taking out her guitar, begins at once to teach the children to sing. This is demonstrated in the utterly captivating "Do-Re-Mi." The children take to the singing immediately — and even more to Maria. They quickly come to trust her, to rely upon her; and when, during her first night with them, there is a noisy thunderstorm, they come creeping into her room, singly and in pairs, and she comforts them with the joyous yodeling tale of "The Lonely Goatherd" (for which, in the motion picture version, "My Favorite Things" is appropriately substituted).

The Captain, meanwhile, has become engaged to marry Frau Elsa Schraeder, a chic and charming widow from Vienna. Visiting her fiance's home, she is entranced by the seven stepchildren she is about to acquire, largely because of the music and manners their new governess has taught them. The Captain, too, is won over. Maria makes him realize how important it is that he should learn to know and love his children, whom, until now, he has treated like members of a well-drilled crew. He throws away his whistle and even joins in as they sing "The Sound Of Music." He now knows he has Maria to thank for bringing the warmth back into his heart.

It is at a party given by the Captain to introduce Frau Schraeder to his neighbors that he and Maria suddenly realize they have fallen in love. Partly to restore some gaiety to the affair, the Captain and Maria demonstrate for his elder son how the "Laendler" should be danced, and it is then that they both realize how much they mean to each other. Horror-struck, Maria packs her few belongings and slips away to the Abbey. But upon her return, the Mother Abbess tells her she must face her problems. She must go back and find the true end of her story. The Mother Abbess encourages the frightened girl with the brave advice to "Climb Ev'ry Mountain."

In Act II events move very quickly. Because Elsa is unwilling to share the dangers incurred by the Captain's defiance of the Nazis, she and the Captain gently release each other from the engagement. And when Maria returns, avowing her love for Georg, they are quietly married at the Abbey. But the Captain has had many demands from the new government to return to service, a political act abhorrent to him. He and his family make their escape during a music festival in Salzburg at which the Trapp Family Singers win a prize for their rendition of "Edelweiss" (the last song lyrics written by Oscar Hammerstein 2nd). By prearrangement, the family slips out of the theatre and into a bus bound for the Abbey. There they hide themselves while a Nazi searching party tries to find them and take them into custody. It is through the final intervention of the young Nazi, Rolf Gruber, whose budding love affair with the eldest Trapp girl softens his heart, that the family eludes their pursuers. When we last see them, they are making good their escape over a high hill near the Abbey as all the sisters wish them well in a last reprise of "Climb ev'ry mountain . . . till you find your dream."

The critiques were as follows:

Brooks Atkinson—*New York Times*

". . . The best of **The Sound of Music** is Rodgers and Hammerstein in good form. Mr. Rodgers has not written with such freshness of style since **The King And I.** Mr. Hammerstein has contributed lyrics that also have the sentiment and dexterity of his best work . . . It is disappointing to see the American musical stage succumbing to the cliches of operetta. The revolution of the Forties and Fifties has lost its fire. But the play retains some of the treasures of those golden days — melodies, rapturous singing and Mary Martin. The sound of music is always moving. Occasionally it is also glorious."

Walter Kerr—*New York Herald Tribune*

". . . The show is handsome, it has a substantial plot, and it is going to be popular . . . But before the play is halfway through its promising chores it becomes not only too sweet for words but almost too sweet for music . . . The people on stage have all melted long before our hearts do. The upshot? What might have been an impressive and moving entertainment will be most admired by people who have always found Sir James M. Barrie pretty rough stuff."

MY FAVORITE THINGS

Lyrics by
OSCAR HAMMERSTEIN II

Secondo (𝄢)

Music by
RICHARD RODGERS

MY FAVORITE THINGS

Lyrics by
OSCAR HAMMERSTEIN II

Music by
RICHARD RODGERS

Primo

6

Secondo(𝄢)

Primo(𝄞)

DO-RE-MI

Lyrics by
OSCAR HAMMERSTEIN II

Secondo (𝄢)

Music by
RICHARD RODGERS

DO-RE-MI

Lyrics by
OSCAR HAMMERSTEIN II

Primo

Music by
RICHARD RODGERS

With spirit

Secondo(𝄢)

poco a poco cresc.

Primo(𝄞)

poco a poco cresc.

f

mf

1.

2.

mf

SIXTEEN GOING ON SEVENTEEN

Lyrics by
OSCAR HAMMERSTEIN II

Secondo

Music by
RICHARD RODGERS

SIXTEEN GOING ON SEVENTEEN

Lyrics by
OSCAR HAMMERSTEIN II

Primo 𝄞

Music by
RICHARD RODGERS

Secondo(𝄢)

Primo(𝄞)

EDELWEISS

Lyrics by
OSCAR HAMMERSTEIN II

Secondo

Music by
RICHARD RODGERS

Edelweiss

Primo

Lyrics by
OSCAR HAMMERSTEIN II

Music by
RICHARD RODGERS

Secondo(𝄢)

Primo

CLIMB EV'RY MOUNTAIN

Lyrics by
OSCAR HAMMERSTEIN II

Secondo ($9\colon$)

Music by
RICHARD RODGERS

With deep feeling, like a prayer

con pedal

Climb Ev'ry Mountain

Lyrics by
OSCAR HAMMERSTEIN II

Primo

Music by
RICHARD RODGERS

With deep feeling, like a prayer

22

Secondo(𝄢)

8va

23

Primo(𝄞)

THE LONELY GOATHERD

Lyrics by
OSCAR HAMMERSTEIN II

Secondo (9:)

Music by
RICHARD RODGERS

THE LONELY GOATHERD

Lyrics by
OSCAR HAMMERSTEIN II

Primo

Music by
RICHARD RODGERS

Secondo(𝄢)

Primo

AN ORDINARY COUPLE

Lyrics by
OSCAR HAMMERSTEIN II

Secondo(𝄢)

Music by
RICHARD RODGERS

AN ORDINARY COUPLE

Lyrics by
OSCAR HAMMERSTEIN II

Primo

Music by
RICHARD RODGERS

30

Secondo($\mathbf{9}$)

no pedal

con pedal

rit.   dim.

Primo

MARIA

Lyrics by
OSCAR HAMMERSTEIN II

Secondo (𝄢)

Music by
RICHARD RODGERS

MARIA

Lyrics by
OSCAR HAMMERSTEIN II

Primo

Music by
RICHARD RODGERS

Lively

34

Secondo(𝄢)

Primo(𝄞)

SO LONG, FAREWELL

Lyrics by
OSCAR HAMMERSTEIN II

Secondo (𝄢)

Music by
RICHARD RODGERS

Moderato

So Long, Farewell

Lyrics by
OSCAR HAMMERSTEIN II

Primo

Music by
RICHARD RODGERS

Secondo (𝄢)

Lively

Primo(𝄞)

40

Secondo (𝄢)

Primo

Much slower

Secondo (𝄢)

Primo(𝄞)

THE SOUND OF MUSIC

Lyrics by
OSCAR HAMMERSTEIN II

Secondo ($\mathbf{9}^{:}$)

Music by
RICHARD RODGERS

THE SOUND OF MUSIC

Lyrics by
OSCAR HAMMERSTEIN II

Primo

Music by
RICHARD RODGERS

Secondo(𝄢)

Primo

RICHARD RODGERS & OSCAR HAMMERSTEIN II